# The Cat Lovers Companion

**Author's Acknowledgement**

A special thank you to my husband Denys for the patience, understanding and whole-hearted support which, as ever, he gave to me during the writing and compilation of this book.

**Managing Editor:** Jo Finnis

**Design:** Paul Turner and Sue Pressley, Stonecastle Graphics Ltd

**Captions:** Louise Houghton

**Typesetting:** DSP, Maidstone, Kent.

**Photographs:** Cogis Agency – Annette Amblin; Bernard Bernic; Philippe Garguil; Jean-Claude Gissey; Jean-Michel Labat; Gérard Lacz; Yves Lanceau; Sylvie Lepage; François Nicaise; Hervé Nicolle; Gérald Potier, François Varin; Serge Vedic; Frank Vidal; Paola Visintini

**Illustrations:** Pam Martins; Terry Burton courtesy of Bernard Thornton Artists, London (astrological portraits)

**Production:** Ruth Arthur; Sally Connolly; Andrew Whitelaw; Neil Randles

**Director of Production:** Gerald Hughes

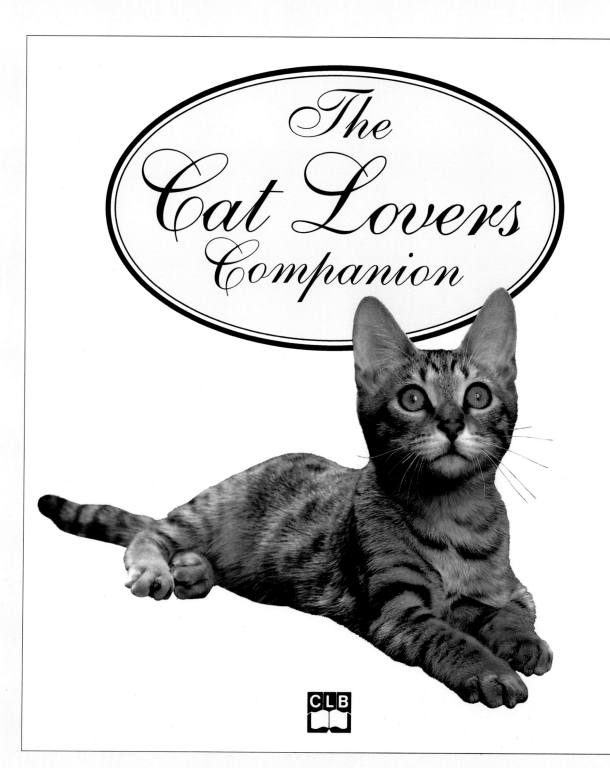

# The Cat Lovers Companion

CLB

# ~ *Introduction* ~

*The Cat Lover's Companion* is for all those who have known and have loved the cat. An intriguing treasury of fascinating feline fact and fable, recounting details of historical cats; heroic cats; famous people and their cats; cat breeds whose myth and origin reach back into the mists of time; superstitions; little-known legends about the cat and a keenly observed astrological section enabling the cat lover to better understand the vagaries of pussy's behaviour! This unique book is also a delightful way in which to 'cat'alogue the birthdays of family, friends and felines, anniversaries and special days to remember.

Exquisitely presented and illustrated throughout, *The Cat Lover's Companion* will be a joy to give or to receive and certainly to cherish, forever…

*The 'Sacred Cat of Burma,' the Birman is distinguished by four white gloves.*

# *~ January ~*

'Refined and delicate natures understand the cat. Women, poets, and artists hold it in great esteem, for they recognise the exquisite delicacy of its nervous system; indeed, only coarse natures fail to discern the natural distinction of the cat.'

Les Chats, Champfleury, 1885

*The intuitive January cat can be a loyal and trustworthy companion.*

# ~ *January* ~

~ 1 ~

~ 2 ~

**SUPERSTITIOUS CATS**

*A cat is very often kept as a lucky mascot in the theatre and disaster strikes any actor who dares to kick it!*

~ 3 ~

~ 4 ~

~ 5 ~

**CATS WITH CONNECTIONS**

*White Heather belonged to Queen Victoria (1819 - 1901). Reminding the Queen of her beloved Scotland, White Heather lived at Buckingham Palace and on surviving Victoria's death, was 'adopted' by her successor, King Edward VII.*

~ 6 ~

~ 7 ~

**CAT SNIPS**

*Probably the only legend surrounding the British wild cat emanates from the county of Leicestershire where there was a cave named 'Black Annis's Bower'. Annis was a wild and terrible woman - sometimes said to be one Agnes Scott, a murderous female thief. In any event, Annis was likened to Britain's only wild carnivore, the wild cat, and she would lie in wait on the branch of an oak tree, springing on her victims below to suck their blood and tear them to pieces with her formidable claws. The legend of Black Annis persisted until the nineteenth century when Leicestershire mill girls bestowed upon her the name of Cat Anna 'the witch who lived in the cellars under the Castle'.*

*The American Shorthair, a handsome breed.*

*American Shorthairs are strong, muscular cats seen in many colours and coat patterns.*

# ~ January ~

~ 8 ~

~ 9 ~

~ 10 ~

~ 11 ~

~ 12 ~

~ 14 ~

**CARTOON CATS**

*Krazy Kat was the first cartoon cat, appearing as a Hearst newspaper strip cartoon drawn by George Herriman in 1910. In 1921 Krazy Kat moved to the silent movie screen where he starred in 'Krazy Kat and Ignatz Mouse'.*

**RECORD-BREAKING CATS**

*Probably the oldest known female cat was Ma, from Devon, who was 34 when she died in 1957.*

**CAT LEGENDS**

*There is a legend that many little kittens were thrown into a river to drown. The mother cat wept and was so distraught that the willows on the bank felt compassion and held out their branches to the struggling kittens. The little kittens clung to them and were saved. Ever since that time, each Spring, the willow wears grey buds that feel as soft and silky as the coats of little kittens. Thus, these trees were called 'pussy willows'.*

*Ragdolls are an enchanting American breed*

*Abyssinians produce on average 4 in a litter. Lively kittens grow into active, intelligent adults.*

# ~ January ~

## ~ 15 ~

## ~ 16 ~

## ~ 17 ~

## ~ 18 ~

## ~ 19 ~

## ~ 20 ~

## ~ 21 ~

### CAT SNIPS
In England at the beginning of the 18th century, bounties were being paid out of parish funds to the killers of the wild cat (felis silvestris). This was designated at four pence a head, considerably cheaper than that paid out for the wolf two centuries earlier, which was fixed at five shillings a head.

### PERSONALITY CATS
*Sir Compton Mackenzie*
*(b. 1883 - d. 1972)*
Well-known British author born in West Hartlepool on the North East coast of England and elder brother of the actress Fay Compton. For many years the President of the Siamese Cat Club, right up to his death, Sir Compton showed an extraordinary devotion towards Siamese cats.

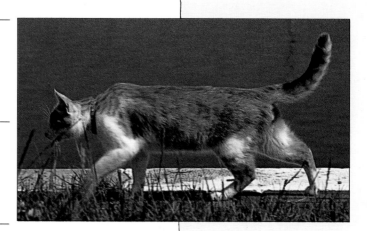

*Stalking on the boardwalk.*

### CAT STARS
Orangey was a sensational motion picture and television personality. A veritable orange 'tiger' which made its cinematic debut in the title role of 'Rhubarb' (1952) and won the Patsy Award in 1952 and 1962. Orangey also appeared in 'Gigot', 'Breakfast at Tiffany's' and in the television series 'Our Miss Brookes'.

*A cat with an agouti coat (when each hair is of two or three different colours) is well camouflaged in the undergrowth.*

~ 22 ~

### SUPERSTITIOUS CATS
Never kick a cat or you will get rheumatism; never drown one or the devil will get you. Throughout the world it is considered to be bad luck to maltreat a cat. This worldwide respect for the cat is probably rooted in those ancient religions in which the cat was a sacred animal and where retribution would befall those who harmed it.

~ 23 ~

~ 24 ~

~ 25 ~

~ 26 ~

~ 27 ~

### PERSONALITY CATS
**Lewis Carroll**
*(b. 27th January 1832 - d. 14th January 1898)*
Born Charles Lutwidgwe Dodgson at Daresbury in the county of Cheshire, as Lewis Carroll he was the author of Alice in Wonderland and Alice Through the Looking Glass. The former features the famous Cheshire Cat who had an uncomfortable habit of slowly disappearing - its smile being the last part to go!

~ 28 ~

### PERSONALITY CATS
**Desmond Morris DPhil.**
*(b. 24th January 1928)*
Zoologist, anthropologist, former Head of the Granada TV and Film Unit at the Zoological Society of London and then Curator of Mammals at London Zoo, Desmond Morris is now an author and presenter of many television programmes specialising in cats, dogs, horses and others. Growing up in the Wiltshire countryside, Desmond lived alongside many working cats and thereafter, cats have played an important role in his life.

Following the success of his book The Naked Ape, the Morris family went to live on the island of Malta where they were adopted by 'a delightful cat' named Nimmo. They later returned to live in England and following a trip to Africa to observe the 'big cats', they found in their garden a little black cat at the top of the apple tree, 'screaming its head off'. They said hello in Swahili - which is Jambo, rescued the cat and adopted him. Jambo became his name and he stayed with the Morris family until his death twelve years later. Entirely black except for a tuft of white on his chest, Jambo was the source of Desmond's more serious observations which led to his best-selling books Catwatching and Catlore.

*Cats are undeniably mysterious creatures.*

*The dense coat of the British Shorthair accentuates the handsome solidity for which it is known.*

~ 29 ~

~ 30 ~

~ 31 ~

*The Egyptian Mau is an exquisite breed that may be either Smoke, Pewter, Silver or Bronze in colour, but always it has the distinctive broken barred and spotted coat pattern.*

## MYTHS & ORIGINS

### The Egyptian Mau

*In the beginning, the wild cat (felis vereata maniculata) was domesticated and the Egyptians called it Mau. This cat was greatly admired for its virility, ferocity and agility and was sacred to the goddess Bast or Bastet - the centre of whose cult was Bubastis on the Eastern Delta of the Nile. A fragment of papyrus from the XVIII Dynasty of Ancient Egypt, dated around 1500 BC, states that the male cat is Ra himself and that he was called Mau because of the speech of the god Sa who said: 'He is like unto that which he hath made, therefore did the name of Ra become Mau'. Accompanying the text is a painting of a cat holding a knife in one paw and the head of a slain serpent in the other. Yet another myth tells of the 'Great Cat of the Persea Tree' killing the great serpent Apep.*

*Throughout the Bubastite Dynasty, the cat superseded all other animaux-derived religions and the cat goddess Bastet absorbed or smothered all rivals to and in the cult. In the domestic situation, the Mau was the subject of home worship whilst enjoying the role of adored pet, frequently adorned with jewelled necklaces and gold earrings. Favourite daughters in Ancient Egypt were often given pet names which meant 'little cat' or 'kitten', or more specifically, 'Mai-sheri' meaning Pussy. In the 1950's, the Egyptian Mau, the only natural breed of spotted domestic cat, was seen at a cat show in Rome by a Princess Troubetsky. The Princess took one home with her to the US and though immediate interest was shown, it was not until 1977 that the CFF (Cat Fanciers Federation) recognised the Egyptian Mau.*

*This Bronze Egyptian Mau possesses the breed's rounded wedge head, luminous green eyes and fine chin.*

# ~ *February* ~

'Seraphita remained for long hours immobile on a cushion, not sleeping, following with her eyes with an extreme intensity of attention, scenes invisible to simple mortals… Her elegance, her distinction, aroused the idea of aristocracy; within her race, she was at least a duchess! She doted on perfumes; with little spasms of pleasure she bit handkerchieves impregnated with scent, she wandered among flasks on the dressing-table… and, if she had been allowed to, would willingly have worn powder!'

La Ménagerie Intime, Théophile Gautier, 1850

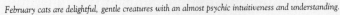

*February cats are delightful, gentle creatures with an almost psychic intuitiveness and understanding.*

# ~ *February* ~

~ 1 ~

~ 2 ~

~ 3 ~

~ 4 ~

~ 5 ~

~ 6 ~

~ 7 ~

## SUPERSTITIOUS CATS

Matagots or magician cats were said to bring wealth to the home where they are well-fed. According to French legend, a matagot must be lured by a plump chicken, then carried home without the prospective owner once looking backwards. Then, at each meal, the matagot must be given the first mouthful of food. In return, it will give its owner a gold coin each morning. In England, Dick Whittington's cat was a matagot who brought its owner good fortune and changed his luck from bad to good.

## PERSONALITY CATS

**Frank Muir CBE**
*(b. 5th February 1920)*
Formerly partnered with Denis Norden, English TV and radio comedy scriptwriter and presenter Frank Muir owns two cats, one called Cinto and the other, Kettering. Each are named after places. Cinto, an Abyssinian, was so-called after the highest mountain range in Corsica, where Frank Muir has a home. Brown Burmese Kettering took his name from the Northamptonshire town.

The Abyssinian has a ticked (agouti) coat.

## PERSONALITY CATS

**Dora Bryan**
*(b. 7th February 1924)*
Associated with Lancashire and first appearing in pantomime in Manchester in 1935, Dora Bryan is a well-known British comedy and character actress - and cat lover. Recently the star of Hello Dolly and 70 Girls 70 on the London stage.

The Abyssinian, much admired for its slendour grace, shows a likeness to the wild cat, felis lybica.

# ~ February ~

## CAT SNIPS

The artist and author of Nonsense Verse, Edward Lear (1812 - 1888), was devoted to Foss, his tabby cat. So much so that when he decided to move house to San Remo in Italy, he instructed the architect to design a replica of his old home - so that the routine of tabby cat Foss should not be disturbed and so be caused the minimum of distress at the move. Lear's drawings of striped tabby cat Foss are well-known, one instance being in those which accompany his rhyme The Owl and the Pussy Cat.

~ 8 ~

~ 9 ~

~ 10 ~

~ 11 ~

~ 12 ~

## PRESIDENTIAL CATS

Born in 1809, Abraham Lincoln came to Presidential Office accompanied by Tabby, a cat belonging to his son, Tad Lincoln.

~ 13 ~

~ 14 ~

Like an owl, the cat watches.

## CAT SNIPS

'The cat is the animal to whom the Creator gave the biggest eye, the softest fur, the most supremely delicate nostrils, a mobile ear, an unrivalled paw and a curved claw borrowed from the rose-tree…'

Colette

## PERSONALITY CATS

**Kim Novak**
(b. 13th February 1933)
Born in Chicago Illinois, American film actress Kim Novak is famous for her starring role as the witch in the film Bell Book and Candle (1959), whose familiar was a seal point Siamese cat called Pyewacket.

*The Abyssinian, much admired for its slender grace, shows a likeness to the wild cat, felis lybica.*

# ~ February ~

## ~ 15 ~

## ~ 16 ~

### CAT STARS
*Pepper, a grey cat who lived in Hollywood, was a true motion picture 'old-timer' and worked alongside such classic movie greats as Charlie Chaplin, Fatty Arbuckle and the Keystone Kops.*

## ~ 17 ~

### CARTOON CATS
*Garfield, the fat lazy cartoon cat was created by Jim Davis in 1978. Within four years Garfield was appearing in nearly a thousand newspaper comic strips worldwide.*

*Kitten and natural 'scratching post.*

## ~ 18 ~

## ~ 19 ~

## ~ 20 ~

## ~ 21 ~

*Just remember … curiosity killed the cat.*

*Fastidious in their personal cleanliness, cats learn very young how to keep themselves in pristine condition.*

## ~ 22 ~

## ~ 23 ~

### SUPERSTITIOUS CATS

*In Scotland in 1590, the witch John Fian and other members of his coven, were charged with having raised or attempted to raise a storm, so as to drown King James VI of Scotland (and the First of England) then returning from Denmark. Fian and his accomplices used cats, by flinging them into the sea, to effect their devilish purpose.*

## ~ 24 ~

*The eyes reflect a cat's health.*

## ~ 25 ~

### CAT FACTS

*The Greeks do not appear to have shown much interest in cats. The Romans, on the other hand, were extremely interested in them and it was Caesar's legions that were largely responsible for introducing cats to the rest of Europe - and particularly to Britain. In the 4th century AD the domestic cat ousted the stone-marten in Rome as a rat-killer. In France, the genet was the animal used in this role until it was supplanted by the cat in the 15th century.*

### CAT SNIPS

*Harry Cat, in the three books of that name by George Seldon, lived in a drainpipe in New York's Times Square station with his pal, Tucker Mouse.*

## ~ 26 ~

## ~ 27 ~

## ~ 28/29 ~

*A cat on a healthy diet should never have any problems with its teeth or gums.*

# ~ *March* ~

*'I conceived the idea that it would be well to hold Cat Shows, so that different breeds, colours, markings etc might be more carefully attended to, and the domestic cat sitting in front of the fire would then possess a beauty and an attractiveness to its owner, unobserved and unknown because uncultivated before.'*

Our Cats, Harrison Weir, 1889

Harrison Weir organised the first cat show
in London at the Crystal Palace in 1871

*The March cat is peace-loving and gentle and may seem to be in a world of his own for much of the time.*

# ~ March ~

## ~ 1 ~

## ~ 2 ~

**CARTOON CATS**
The 'Cat in the Hat' was a fictional character created by Dr. Seuss and first appeared in 'The Cat in the Hat' in 1957.

## ~ 3 ~

## ~ 4 ~

**SUPERSTITIOUS CATS**
In what was known as Bohemia, in western Czechoslovakia, the cat is regarded as a symbol of fertility and one buried in a field of grain will guarantee a good harvest.

## ~ 5 ~

## ~ 6 ~

## ~ 7 ~

**PERSONALITY CATS**

***Charles Baudelaire***
*(b. 1821 - d. 1869)*
This 19th century French writer fully understood the mystique of the feline race when he said: '…chat mystérieux, chat séraphique, chat étrange…'

Considered to be an eccentric in his complete empathy with every cat he met, Baudelaire devoted several poems to them in Fleurs du Mal, often felt that the cat was a spirit or divinity which reigned over the household and asked: 'Peut-être est-il fée, est-il dieu ?' ('Perhaps he is a spirit, or god ?')

*The Blue Russian's incomparable good looks.*

*Bright green, almond-shaped eyes, medium blue coats tipped with silver and small feet distinguish the Russian Blue.*

# ~ March ~

~ 8 ~

**CAT SNIPS**

*Chinese legend maintains that the cat is the product of a lioness and a monkey - the lioness endowing her offspring with dignity and the monkey, with curiosity and playfulness.*

~ 9 ~

## PERSONALITY CATS

**Rt. Hon. the Lord Wilson of Rievaulx**
*(b. 11th March 1916)*
*Well-known as Harold Wilson, a former Prime Minister of Great Britain and Labour Member of Parliament for Huyton, Liverpool. Mr. Wilson and his writer wife Mary owned Nemo, a seal point Siamese male who always accompanied them on their holiday trips to the Scilly Isles, off the coast of Cornwall.*

## SUPERSTITIOUS CATS

*The Japanese prefer their own native short-tailed cat - the Japanese Bobtail - because they are less likely to 'bewitch' humans. Japanese sailors have long taken tri-coloured or me'kay cats on their ships to bring them good luck. The figure of a cat with its left paw raised is commonly seen in gift shops in that country, where they are sold as souvenirs. It is believed that the beckoning cat brings good fortune to its owner.*

~ 10 ~

~ 11 ~

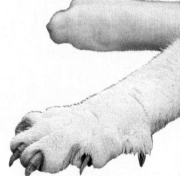

~ 12 ~

~ 13 ~

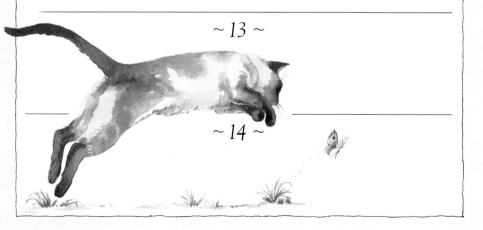

~ 14 ~

*A delicate Japanese Bobtail. This colouring in the breed, known as Mi-Ke, is said to bring good fortune.*

*A unique and endearing characteristic of the cat is its purr, commonly thought to convey contentment, but unproven.*

# ~ March ~

~ 15 ~

~ 16 ~

~ 17 ~

~ 18 ~

~ 19 ~

~ 20 ~

~ 21 ~

**CAT FACTS**

Around 450 BC, anyone who killed a cat in Egypt was punished by death. It was also customary in Ancient Egypt, in the case of fire, to save the domestic cat before any attempt was made to put out the flames. When a cat died the whole family would shave off their eyebrows as a sign of mourning.

**CAT SNIPS**

The musical 'Cats', produced by Andrew Lloyd Webber and based on Old Possum's Book of Practical Cats by TS Eliot, is the longest-running musical ever performed in London's West End. It first opened at the New London Theatre on 11th May 1981 and since has been performed in thirteen countries and translated into ten different languages.

The Ragdoll originates from California.

The Ragdoll, so named for its unique ability to relax completely when handled.

# ~ March ~

## ~ 22 ~

### CAT STARS
*Pyewacket was a movie star cat who won the Patsy Award for his role in 'Bell, Book and Candle' (1959) in which he starred with Kim Novak, James Stewart, Jack Lemmon and Ernie Kovacs.*

## ~ 23 ~

## ~ 24 ~

### CAT SNIPS
*Benignus, the large red cat belonging to author Eleanor Farjeon, was particularly possessive towards his mistress and would spit at all who visited the house. Children's author Eleanor Farjeon (1881 - 1965) was a devoted cat lover and enthused that one special feline 'was the reason that all Egypt knew cat worship'.*

## ~ 25 ~

## ~ 26 ~

## ~ 27 ~

## ~ 28 ~

*The Persian, King of the cats.*

### PERSONALITY CATS

**Sir Dirk Bogarde**
*(b. 28th March 1921)*
*Knighted in 1992, Dirk Bogarde is a British actor who, early in his film career was famous for his role as Dr. Simon Sparrow in the series of 'Doctor' films. Graduating to more dramatic performances in such movies as The Spanish Gardener and latterly, Death in Venice, Dirk Bogarde has been a life-long cat lover and is deeply interested in its mysticism.*

*Occurring in Chinchilla Longhair litters for many years, the Golden Persian as a breed gained UK recognition in 1983.*

# ~ March ~

~ 29 ~

~ 30 ~

~ 31 ~

*A Birman kitten's miaow is music to any cat lover's ear.*

## MYTHS & ORIGINS

### Birman

Long before the teachings of Buddha enlightened the peoples of Asia, a temple was built high on the slopes of Mount Lugh by the Khmer tribe who lived in western Burma. The temple was called Lao Tsun and it was here that the Kittah priests worshipped the golden, blue-eyed goddess Tsun-Kyan-Kse, to whose care the transmigration of souls was entrusted. The temple was guarded by many white longhaired cats with yellow eyes into whose bodies, according to legend, passed the souls of dead priests.

One such cat, whose name was Sinh, was the personal favourite of the High Priest Mun-Ha. One day, as Mun-Ha knelt to pray before the statue of the golden goddess, he was killed by invaders. Sinh leapt upon the body of his master and looked up into the sapphire eyes of the goddess. At that moment, the soul of the priest entered the body of the cat whose fur immediately took on the golden glow of the goddess and its eyes became a brilliant blue to match her own. Sinh's nose, ears, legs and tail darkened to take on the colour of the earth but his paws, resting on the body of his dead master, remained pure white as a symbol of purity. Thus the Birman or, the Sacred Cat of Burma, came into being.

*Birmans have brilliant blue eyes.*

*Both good natured and beautiful, the Birman is an ideal house pet that gets on well with other animals.*

# ~ *April* ~

*'The male cat is Ra himself, and he was called Mau because of the speech of the god Sa, who said concerning him: "He is like unto that which he hath made, therefore did the name of Ra become Mau".'*

Written on a fragment of papyrus from the XVIII Dynasty
of Ancient Egypt, c.1500 BC

*The April cat bursts with vitality and curiosity and therefore may be difficult to get in at night.*

# ~ April ~

**CAT FACTS**

*The Chinese knew the domestic cat before Europeans had ever heard of it. The Japanese were not far behind them. In China and Japan the cat was used to protect the silkworms from rodents and Confucius himself was reported to have owned a cat of which he was very fond.*

~ 1 ~

~ 2 ~

~ 3 ~

~ 4 ~

~ 5 ~

*The Somali retains some wild characteristics.*

**SUPERSTITIOUS CATS**

*Sailors believe that if a ship's cat mews and appears to be cross, they will face a hard voyage - but if it is bright and lively, there will be a brisk 'following' wind. It used to be said that a contrary wind at sea could be raised by shutting a cat in a canister. Throwing a cat overboard resulted in an immediate storm. No sailor would dream of doing this, however, since it was considered good luck to have a cat on board.*

~ 6 ~

~ 7 ~

**CAT SNIPS**

*Mr. Mistopheles was the original conjuring cat from TS Eliot's 'Old Possum's Book of Practical Cats'. A small, quiet black cat, he managed to produce seven kittens out of a hat!*

*The Somali is a long-haired Abyssinian sharing all its characteristics, except in the voice which is very quiet.*

# ~ April ~

## ~ 8 ~

## ~ 9 ~

## ~ 10 ~

**CAT STARS**

*Tonto was a fictional character from the 1974 film of the same name in which he makes a trip across America with his owner Harry, an elderly New York widower.*

## ~ 11 ~

## ~ 12 ~

**SUPERSTITIOUS CATS**

*It is said that in the southern regions of France, if a young unmarried girl accidentally steps on a cat's tail, she will have to wait twelve months before she finds a husband.*

## ~ 13 ~

## ~ 14 ~

**CAT SNIPS**

*Edgar Allan Poe (1809 - 1849), author of the macabre Tales of Mystery and Imagination, was devoted to his tortoiseshell cat Catarina. Poverty stricken and unable to afford sufficient heat for his wife who lay dying of consumption, Poe placed Catarina on the bed to keep his wife warm. The cat obligingly - or most probably mindful of its own comfort - stayed with the sick woman and, inspired by its loyalty, Poe was moved to write one of his best-known tales, The Black Cat.*

*The Burmese, proud and full of grace.*

*These Abyssinian kittens display the breed's large tufted ears, rounded wedge-shaped heads and large, almond-shaped eyes.*

## ~ 15 ~

## ~ 16 ~

## ~ 17 ~

### CAT SNIPS

*Non-pedigree cats generally live longer than pedigree cats. However, one pedigree cat reached its 31st birthday on the 17th April in 1989. This was Sukoo, a seal point Siamese who lived in Devon in the South of England and who was thought to be the oldest living pedigree cat on record.*

## ~ 18 ~

### CAT SNIPS

*Naval hero cat Simon belonged to the Captain of HMS Amethyst and on 20th April 1949, when the Chinese Communists bombarded the ship with gunfire on the Yangtse River, the Captain and many other crew members were killed. Sturdy black and white Simon however, wounded and with whiskers singed, endeavoured to kill off the rats disturbed by the shellfire, which then rampaged through the ship. His prodigious catches were duly recorded by the remaining crew and on reaching Hong Kong, they found that Simon's fame had spread before him as he was greeted with letters, presents and telegrams of congratulations. Following his return to Britain, Simon pined away and died and posthumously was awarded the Dickin Medal, the animal equivalent to the Victoria Cross, for showing outstanding courage in the face of adversity during that historic occasion in 1949.*

## ~ 19 ~

## ~ 20 ~

## ~ 21 ~

### PERSONALITY CATS

**Sir Kingsley Amis**
*(b. 16th April 1922)*
*Author, poet and intellectual, Kingsley Amis, shares his London home with Sarah Snow, a graceful white cat with pale green eyes. With just slightly less than a semi-long coat, and a hint of Angora in her ancestry, Sarah Snow enjoys the run of the house and is a gentle soul who likes to sit in the sun or doze by the radiator.*

*Author of such classics as Lucky Jim and The Old Devils, for which he won the Booker Prize for Fiction in 1986, Kingsley Amis has lived surrounded by pets throughout his life - mainly both cats and dogs. Respecting a cat with intelligence, the author says that 'cats aren't as stupid as they often seem'. Sarah Snow is obviously a cat in this category and her master has written poems about their conversations. Despite venturing under floorboards with typical feline inquisitiveness and digging in her claws when sitting on her master's lap, Sarah Snow and Sir Kingsley Amis remain the very best of friends.*

*A threatening pose with bristling whiskers.*

# ~ The Cat Lover's Companion ~

A cat will get lonely if left for any length of time so a companion is often a good idea.

# ~ April ~

## ~ 22 ~

### RECORD-BREAKING CATS
*The largest recorded cat in Britain was a male called Poppa who died in 1985 weighing 20kgs (44lbs). He lived in Gwent in Wales and his average daily food intake consisted of one and a half tins of cat food, one tin of evaporated milk, two handfuls of cat biscuits, potatoes, cabbage, carrots, gravy and home-made sponge cake.*

## ~ 23 ~

## ~ 24 ~

## ~ 25 ~

### CAT SNIPS
*A black cat named Eponine was the pampered feline companion of author Théophile Gautier. Pretty Eponine dined at table with her master, partaking first of soup and then of fish, with all the delicacy of a well-mannered child.*

## ~ 26 ~

## ~ 27 ~

## ~ 28 ~

### SUPERSTITIOUS CATS
*In the Middle Ages, cats were not very popular because of their association with witchcraft and black magic. Superstitions about cats, some of them current today, date from this period. There are still people who believe that the cat is a reincarnation of the devil and regard it as bad luck if one crosses their path. In other places the reverse is held to be true, and that a black cat crossing one's path brings good luck.*

*The Bombay has a beautiful coat.*

*Perhaps this pussy is dreaming of going to sea with an owl in a beautiful pea-green boat.*

~ 29 ~

_____

~ 30 ~

_____

### Singapura

*Possibly the smallest of the domestic cats, weighing around 4 - 6kgs (9 - 13lbs), the Singapura is a natural breed which originated on the island of Singapore. A free-ranging cat in its native land, the Singapura with a smooth, shorthaired agouti coat in its 'natural' colours of ivory and brown, sought shelter in the drains of Singapore where it was known as the 'drain cat'. Following its registration with the Singapore Feline Society, the Singapura was imported to America in 1975 and shown in 1976. Though still quite a rare breed, this quiet yet sociable little cat can be seen in various coat colours both in America and less frequently in the UK.*

*Often a solitary creature, the cat is ingenious in his resourcefulness when making up games to play.*

*Known in its native country as the 'Drain Cat', the elegant Singapura is a demure and affectionate cat.*

# ~ *May* ~

*'To gain the friendship of a cat is a difficult thing. The cat is a philosophical, methodical, quiet animal, tenacious of its own habits, fond of order and cleanliness, and it does not lightly confer its friendship. If you are worthy of its affection, a cat will be your friend, but never your slave. He keeps his free will, though he loves, and he will not do for you what he thinks is unreasonable. But if he once gives himself to you it is with absolute confidence and affection!'*

Théophile Gautier, 1850

*May's cat loves his home and his food; the ideal pet for the loyal cat lover.*

# ~ May ~

**CAT STARS**

*Jones was an orange-striped cat that featured in the movie 'Alien' (20th Century Fox, 1979). Jones was one of the two survivors following the attack on the ship Nostromo.*

~ 1 ~

~ 2 ~

~ 3 ~

*A playful rough and tumble.*

**CAT SNIPS**

*Philosopher Sir Isaac Newton, famous for his laws of motion and gravity, was also a confirmed cat lover who was deeply concerned about the welfare of his feline friends. Therefore, so that they should not feel restricted and be at liberty to wander freely in and out of the house when doors were closed, he invented the cat-flap.*

~ 4 ~

~ 5 ~

~ 6 ~

~ 7 ~

**SUPERSTITIOUS CATS**

*A Celtic belief was that kittens born in May were badly behaved and troublesome. In Celtic mythology, the month of May was a time of ill-omen.*

# ~ *The Cat Lover's Companion* ~

*There is a certain sensuous delight in watching a cat at his langorous libations.*

# ~ May ~

## CAT SNIPS

*Sister Smudge was the feline member of Branch 29 of the General Municipal Boilermakers and Allied Trades Union. She was appointed resident cat at the peoples' Palace Museum in Glasgow, Scotland in 1979 to deal with a temporary rodent problem.*

## CAT SNIPS

*Blue point Balinese variant Willow is the current feline of BBC's TV programme Blue Peter. In the care of former Abyssinian breeder Mrs. Edith Menezes, Willow, who was born on 11th May 1986, is exhibited at cat shows throughout the UK and has travelled over 40,000 miles by air to meet her many friends and admirers. Willow follows seal point Siamese Jason and silver Tabbies Jack and Jill as senior pussy cat in residence on the Blue Peter show.*

~ 8 ~

~ 9 ~

~ 10 ~

~ 11 ~

~ 12 ~

~ 13 ~

~ 14 ~

### Burmese & other Asians

*The result of a 'natural' mating, the brown shorthaired cat was and is known in Burma. The first of these 'Burmese' cats was introduced to the Western world in 1930, when a single brown female named Wong Mau arrived in New Orleans in the US, in the company of a sailor. This 'cobby' roundish type of cat was eventually given to a Dr. Joseph C Thompson of San Francisco, who decided to breed from the richly-hued brown feline. Illustrations of the Supalak or Thong Daeng - probable ancestors of the 'foreigns', Burmese, Siamese and the Korat – could be seen in the south-east Asian 'Cat Book Poems', dated between 1350 and 1750. This is possibly the oldest known cat book in existence and reflects the high regard accorded to the cat at that time.*

*Like all kittens, Burmese are irresistible.*

*The Balinese is a long-haired mutation of the Siamese which first appeared in the 1950s.*

# ~ *May* ~

## ~ 15 ~

## ~ 16 ~

### SUPERSTITIOUS CATS

*Occult powers are often attributed to cats. It is said that they also have the power of hypnotism. A cat with three different hues in its coat protects one against fire and fever.*

## ~ 17 ~

## ~ 18 ~

## ~ 19 ~

### CAT SNIPS

*In 1758, the Swedish naturalist Carolus Linnaeus classified the domestic cat as felis catus. Since then, and understandably so, the domestic cat has also been known as felis domesticus. The domestic cat flourished in Ancient Egypt over 2,500 years ago and according to early Sanskrit writings was also found to be in India at around that time.*

## ~ 20 ~

## ~ 21 ~

### PERSONALITY CATS

**James Mason**
*(b. 15th May 1909 - d. 27th July 1984)*
*James Mason was the darkly attractive British film star who acted with Margaret Lockwood during the 'Forties in such classic films as The Man in Grey and The Wicked Lady. A well-known ailurophile and feline benefactor in his home-town of Huddersfield, James Mason and his first wife, screen-writer Pamela Kellino, owned many Siamese cats and several strays. Together they wrote the book The Cats in Our Lives in 1949.*

*Venice is home to many cats.*

# ~ The Cat Lover's Companion ~

For animals known for their hatred of water, the cat has a peculiar affinity with Venice, city of canals.

# ~ May ~

## CARTOON CATS

*Felix the Cat, undoubtedly one of the most famous cats in animated films, started his career in 'Feline Follies' (1919), an animated feature produced by Pat Sullivan, an Australian cartoonist for Paramount. Felix inspired the popular 1920's song 'Felix Kept on Walking'. Felix was revived in 1960 by Joe Orilo in a television series of 260 episodes.*

## PERSONALITY CATS

### Sir Walter Scott
#### (1771 - 1832)

*Scottish poet, novelist, editor and critic and Deputy Sheriff of Selkirk in 1799, just a few of Sir Walter Scott's better-known books are Guy Mannering, Rob Roy, Redgauntlet and The Talisman. Absorbed in folklore and the supernatural, Scott was devoted to cats and the portrait by John Watson Gordon shows the author at work at his desk with Hinx, his tabby cat lying close by. On the subject which fascinated him most, Scott intuitively wrote: 'Cats are a mysterious kind of folk. There is more passing in their minds than we are aware of.'*

~ 22 ~

~ 23 ~

~ 24 ~

## CAT SNIPS

*Two of the most commonly used names for cats in England during the Middle Ages were Pyewacket and Grimalkin, the latter meaning 'little grey man'. Matthew Hopkins, self-appointed witch-hunter in Cromwellian England, wrote his book 'Discovery of Witches' in 1647. Its frontispiece shows a group of 'familiars' - one of which is a cat named Pyewacket.*

~ 25 ~

~ 26 ~

~ 27 ~

~ 28 ~

*Cats can be very entertaining pets.*

*The Ocicat is well-muscled, graceful and lively with tufted ears and large eyes set in a classic wedge-shaped head.*

# ~ *May* ~

## PRESIDENTIAL CATS

*John F Kennedy, born this day in 1917, was aided by a feline during his time at the White House. Tom Kitten, as he was known, belonged to Caroline Kennedy, the President's daughter, and was the first White House cat since Teddy Roosevelt's Slippers. Tom Kitten died on August 21, 1962.*

~ 29 ~

~ 30 ~

~ 31 ~

## MYTHS & ORIGINS

### *Siamese*

*Legend has it that Siamese cats were kept to serve as repositories in which to keep the transmigrating souls of Siamese Royalty. Residing only in the Royal Palace in Bangkok - hence the earlier name of Royal Palace Cat - it is said that they were the product of a union with an albino domestic cat belonging to the King and an Egyptian, or some say, a black Temple cat. The resulting 'Siamese' were then appointed as guardians of the Temple and closely confined to keep the breed pure. Most early Siamese displayed one, two or three kinks in their tails. Frances Simpson states that 'HM King of Siam prizes most highly the unusual kinked tail of the Siamese cat.' The myth of its origin is that a Royal Siamese princess of long ago, whilst bathing, placed her rings for safekeeping, on the tail of her favourite cat who obligingly 'kinked' it for that purpose !*

*The squint - another inherent Siamese feature - is said to have originated when the priests of ancient Siam set the temple cats to guard a valuable vase. The cats carried out this duty for so long and with so much concentration that their eyes became permanently crossed! In 1884 Mr Owen Gould, the British Consul General in Bangkok, was presented with a pair of Siamese cats by a Royal 'personage'. On his return to England he gave these to his sister, Mrs Veley. A breeding pair, these strangely exciting cats were called Mia and Pho - Siamese for Mother and Father. More imports followed and in 1898, Wankee, stolen from the Royal Palace as a kitten, became the first seal point Siamese to become a Champion on the English showbench.*

*The Balinese cat's favourite food is fish, though this one seems to have a sweet tooth.*

Cool and majestic, the Siamese is as distinctive as it is revered.

# ~ *June* ~

*What does a kitten dream of…?*

*Bright, nodding flowers;*
*Gay butterflies?*
*Sweet-scented grass;*
*Blue summer skies?*

*Cool woodland path*
*And dancing leaves?*
*Sunlight glinting*
*Through tall trees?*

*A puff of down*
*Gently touched by paw,*
*To float up and away*
*'Til seen no more?*

*The dreams of a kitten*
*Are gossamer things -*
*A slight hint of a breeze;*
*A faint rustle of wings…*

*The dreams of a kitten*
*Are too precious to stay,*
*And as the fey mists of time,*
*They must melt away…*

*Anthology of Verse, Joan Moore, 1979*

*The June cat is energetic and intelligent, interested in everything and everyone, he hates being shut in.*

# ~ June ~

A Persian chest as white as snow.

~ 1 ~

**CAT SNIPS**
*Nostradamus, the French astrologer (1503 - 1566), possessed a cat named Grimalkin.*

## PERSONALITY CATS

**Thomas Hardy**
*(b. 2nd June 1840 - d. 11th January 1928)*

Born in Dorset, England, Thomas Hardy, novelist, dramatist, poet and cat lover, was renowned for such literary epics as Children of the New Forest and Tess of the d'Urbevilles. This quiet, gentle countryman was an ardent naturalist and owned many cats during the course of his life. Felines were his passion and at Max Gate, his home in Dorchester, he wrote to his wife Emma who was away from home at the time: 'Kitsey, looking for a bed in which to have her kittens, has been up to the maid's room and has torn her Sunday hat in rents. I have given her 5/- to buy another and she is quite content.'

A number of portraits show Hardy accompanied by a cat and latterly he was given Cobby, a small blue Persian with orange eyes and one of the author's last portraits taken shows him cuddling this kitten. Immediately after the death of Thomas Hardy, it is said that Cobby disappeared and was never found.

~ 2 ~

~ 3 ~

~ 4 ~

**CAT STARS**
*Jake was a fictional character who was also known as 'The Cat From Outer Space' and starred in the movie of that name with Ken Berry, Sandy Duncan and McLean Stevenson (Walt Disney Productions, 1978). Jake was portrayed by a Hollywood feline named Rumpled and arrived on earth in a spaceship which he controlled with his mind - and used his magic collar to keep hapless earthlings out of trouble!*

~ 5 ~

~ 6 ~

~ 7 ~

*The Blue Persian has a sumptuous coat of great length and density, dramatically offset by amber eyes.*

# ~ June ~

## CATS WITH CONNECTIONS

*Wilberforce lived at No. 10 Downing Street under the tenancy of four Prime Ministers. He first moved into No. 10 in 1973, serving under Edward Heath and was still there when Margaret Thatcher came into power. Wilberforce died in 1988.*

~ 8 ~

~ 9 ~

~ 10 ~

*The Oriental has great sophistication.*

~ 11 ~

## SUPERSTITIOUS CATS

*An American hill country superstition says that a cat can decide whether or not a girl should get married. The debating bride-to-be takes three hairs from the cat's tail and wraps them in paper, which she then places under her door step. If in the morning, the cat hairs are arranged in a 'Y' pattern, the answer is 'Yes' but if the hairs form the letter 'N', the answer is 'No'.*

## CAT SNIPS

*'Cats are distant, discreet, impeccably clean and able to stay silent. What more could be needed to be good company?'*

Marie Leczinska (18th century)

~ 12 ~

~ 13 ~

~ 14 ~

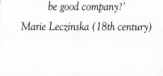

*It is as kittens at play that cats learn the skills of their species for hunting and survival.*

**CAT SNIPS**

*With powerful muscles especially in their hind legs, the domestic cat has been known to reach running speeds of up to 25 mph.*

~ 15 ~

~ 16 ~

~ 17 ~

~ 18 ~

~ 19 ~

~ 20 ~

~ 21 ~

**PERSONALITY CATS**

**Beryl Reid OBE**
(b. 17th June 1920)
*Well-loved English actress, comedienne and devoted cat-lover, Beryl Reid was born in Hereford and educated in Manchester. Famous in the 'Fifties for her radio comedy role of Marlene, the schoolgirl from Birmingham, Beryl Reid has starred in a formidable list of films such as Star, the story of Gertrude Lawrence, The Killing of Sister George, Joe Orton's Entertaining Mr Sloane and many more.*

*Beryl now lives in blissful seclusion in Honeypot Cottage - a pussies' paradise - on the River Thames. Allowed to come and go as they please and all named after people that Beryl has known, are tabby cat Jenny, tri-colour Elsie, the beautiful longhaired Muriel and four 'ginger' cats - Clive, Billy, Paris, and Tufnell. There are also Dimly, a large black, Sir Harry a tabby, a silver tabby called Patrick and brown tabbies Fred and Emma...*

**CAT SNIPS**

*Fred Wunpound RN - bought for the price of £1 from the RSPCA, hence his name - was the mascot and official mouse-catcher aboard HMS Hecate from 1966 - 1974. This redoubtable black and white cat was given ships 'papers' as Able Sea Cat Wunpound F. Cat/00002 and travelled over 250,000 sea miles aboard the 2,800-ton Ocean Survey ship HMS Hecate, during his eight years' service. He held the 'Blue Nose Certificate' for services in Icelandic waters and at Fred's own request was promoted from Able Sea Cat to Leading Sea Cat in 1971.*

*With admirers at every port of call, one Tinkerbelle, a tortie longhair from Surrey, became an ardent fan and sent Fred a Valentine's Day card inscribed: 'To the one and only sea cat, from a very lovely she-cat'. Inspiring many column inches in the world's press, Fred finally 'swallowed the anchor' in 1974 when the introduction of the anti-rabies law prevented animal mascots sailing in HM ships. At Easter 1975 Fred took up residence at the Dr. Barnado's Princess Margaret School in Taunton, Somerset where sadly, on June 15th the following year, he passed away. Fred was buried with full honours in the garden of the School and it is understood that HMS Hecate paid for his headstone.*

*Kittens get into lots of trouble.*

*A queen watches her kitten. By three or four weeks it will be on solids, by two months weaned.*

# ~ June ~

## ~ 22 ~

## ~ 23 ~

### SUPERSTITIOUS CATS

*It is said that to dream of cats is unfavourable as this denotes treachery. In Tasseography - fortune-telling by tea leaves - a cat signifies false friends and deceit; someone lies in treacherous ambush, probably a false friend.*

## ~ 24 ~

## ~ 25 ~

## ~ 26 ~

### CARTOON CATS

*Sylvester, the animated cartoon character first appeared in the 'Life with Feathers' television cartoon in 1945.*

## ~ 27 ~

## ~ 28 ~

*A white Persian is a precious creature.*

# ~ The Cat Lover's Companion ~

*The sleep of a cat is much coveted for its blameless ease and disconcern.*

# ~ June ~

## ~ 29 ~

## ~ 30 ~

### PERSONALITY CATS

#### Ruskin Spear CBE

*(b. 30th June 1911 - d. 9th January 1990)*

*This Royal Academician enjoyed a lively relationship with the cats in his life - they intrigued him and were a constant source of inspiration to him. In his paintings, Oliver was a large, fat black and white featured in 'Cat and Piano' which was exhibited in the 1984 Royal Academy Summer Exhibition. 'Ginger Cat' amongst poppies and daisies, 'Brindle Cat', a huge tabby and white seated at table and 'Black Cat' on a green armchair are other well-known examples of the artist's work.*

*A pretty Norwegian Forest Cat was a constant companion and others, brought in by Spear's wife, filled the house. Black and white blotched Funny Face; Manny, an old feral, found nearby; Trixie and Leo and a 'whole lot more'… Before his death in 1990, Ruskin Spear said: Give me a moggie every time. Pedigrees are cats with birth certificates, aren't they?' The artist was not impressed by pedigree cats and the degree of pomposity which this status implied. An honest-to-goodness moggie was his preference.*

### CAT SNIPS

*'One of the most singular-looking cats was "Russ" of Muscovite origin, whose coat resembled a chinchilla. Another, "Zeyla", who had been captured in Abyssinia during the war, was most remarkable for her woebegone appearance, seemingly discontented at her sudden elevation into notoriety, and longing for her barbaric freedom.'*

The Graphic: 'An afternoon with the Cats (at the Crystal Palace)'

*What dreams of mice and fish stir in the slumbers of these napping cats?*

*When not sleeping, a cat is often grooming, a lengthy process of meticulous care and seriousness.*

# ~ *July* ~

'The Egyptians have observed in the eyes of a Cat, the encrease of the Moonlight for with the Moone, they shine more fully at the full, and more dimly in the change and wain, and the male Cat doth also vary his eyes with the Sunne; for when the Sunne ariseth, the apple of his eye is long; towards noone it is round, and at the evening it cannot be seene at all, but the whole eye sheweth alike.'

*Historie of Foure-footed Beasts*, Edward Topsell, 1607

*The July cat thrives on affection and repays it generously. It makes an excellent parent and devoted pet.*

# ~ July ~

~ 1 ~

~ 2 ~

*The stalking Bombay is formidable.*

### SUPERSTITIOUS CATS
*Many people believe that a black cat brings good fortune and also, that anyone who finds the one perfect, pure white hair in an all-black cat and plucks it out without being scratched, will find great wealth and good luck in love.*

~ 3 ~

~ 4 ~

### CAT FACTS
*Unlike the dog, the cat has no desire to serve any master. Most cats refuse to learn tricks but are often capable of accomplishing quite difficult feats to obtain their own ends!*

### CAT LEGENDS
*Typhon, from whom our word 'typhoon' originates, was a fearsome creature, whose fiery breath caused great destruction in the world when, as was his custom, he roared over land and sea, raising fierce hurricanes that destroyed everything in their path. The tyrant's ambition was to gain sovereignty not only over men, but over the gods also. So nearly did he succeed in attaining his ambition that, for a time, most of the gods and goddesses hid from him in the form of animals. Hecate, a mysterious divinity whom the ancients identified with night and who associated with ghosts and demons and was said to be an expert at magic, adopted the shape of a cat, until Zeus destroyed the giant Typhon with a thunderbolt. Thereafter, though she resumed her proper form, Hecate had a special affection for cats. She became the patron saint of witches - as Shakespeare knew when he made his 'dark and midnight hags' appeal to her for help in ruining Macbeth. So it followed naturally that those who practised witchcraft should also cultivate a liking for cats.*

~ 5 ~

~ 6 ~

~ 7 ~

A 'comfort' of cats. Two of a kind curl up together.

# ~ July ~

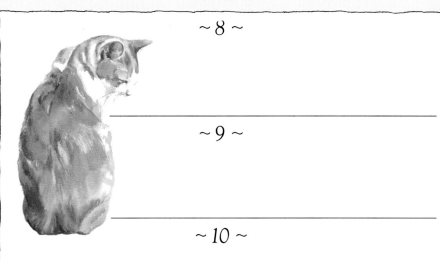

~ 8 ~

~ 9 ~

~ 10 ~

~ 11 ~

~ 12 ~

*Pretty maids all in a row.*

**CAT SNIPS**

*Williamina, a white cat belonging to 19th century British author Charles Dickens, produced a litter of kittens - all except one of which were found homes. Because of its devotion to its master, the remaining kitten was called The Master's Cat. In order to gain attention as the hour grew late, this little cat would snuff out with its paw, the candle which lit the author's desk. Charles Dickens acknowledged the hint and happily complied with a cuddle for his favourite cat!*

**CAT SNIPS**

*The first official Cat Show in Britain took place at the Crystal Palace in London on 13th July 1871. It was organised by writer, artist and cat-lover Harrison Weir.*

~ 13 ~

~ 14 ~

**PRESIDENTIAL CATS**

*Gerald Ford, born this day in 1913, was privileged to have Shan as the first cat of his administration. This was a Siamese and belonged to Susan, President Ford's daughter.*

*The white Shorthair is a most delightful cat, particularly when odd-eyed. The blue-eyed variety can suffer from deafness.*

## PERSONALITY CATS

**Iris Murdoch DBE, CBE**
*(b. 15th July 1919)*
*Best-selling British author Iris Murdoch has had a lifelong interest in cats and has recently published a book entitled Particularly Cats and More Cats, containing an account of the cats she has lived with throughout her life. She now owns one cat named General Butchkin, and entertains a number of visiting strays.*

~ 15 ~

~ 16 ~

~ 17 ~

~ 18 ~

~ 19 ~

### CAT SNIPS

*The average life span of a cat is twelve years and it is said that to compare the age of a cat to that of a human, simply multiply the cat's age by seven.*

~ 20 ~

~ 21 ~

*The Chartreux has orange or copper eyes.*

## PERSONALITY CATS

**Ernest Hemingway**
*(b. 21st July 1898 - d. 2nd July 1961)*
*A former war correspondent covering the Spanish Civil War and later a successful novelist and winner of the 1954 Nobel Prize, Ernest Hemingway latterly had more than thirty cats living at his home in Havana. Earlier, whilst living in Paris, France with his wife and young son, Hemingway would leave F. Puss, his yellow-eyed cat, to baby-sit whilst he and his wife went out. Consternation was rife among friends and neighbours who feared that the cat would lie on the baby and suffocate him. But not F. Puss; the careful cat sat upright and on guard until the return of the Hemingways.*

*With novels such as To Have and To Have Not, The Snows of Kilimanjaro and For Whom the Bell Tolls to his credit - many of which were made into classic movies, Hemingway discussing his favourite subject said: 'The cat has complete emotional honesty - an attribute' he pointed out 'not often found in humans.'*

*Keeping a long-haired cat in perfect condition requires daily grooming and the occasional bath.*

# ~ July ~

## CAT SNIPS

*In New York in 1963, a Chinchilla Persian Longhair called Babyface and a Silver Persian Longhair called Nicodemus were married. The service was conducted by a Beagle and the Matron-of-Honour was another Persian cat.*

~ 22 ~

~ 23 ~

## CAT STARS

*'That Darn Cat' - a fictional feline, portrayed by Syn Cat, star of the Walt Disney film of the same name (1964). He appeared with human stars Dean Jones, Hayley Mills, Roddy McDowell, Frank Gorshin and William Demarest.*

~ 24 ~

~ 25 ~

~ 26 ~

~ 27 ~

~ 28 ~

## PERSONALITY CATS

### Raymond Chandler
*(b. 23rd July 1888 - d. 26th March 1959)*
*Born in Chicago, Illinois, Raymond Chandler, famous for his detective stories featuring private eye Philip Marlowe, created the classic 'detective novel' genre of the 'Thirties and 'Forties - many of which were made into successful films, notably The Big Sleep starring Humphrey Bogart and Lauren Bacall. A lifelong cat devotee, Chandler owned a black Persian named Taki, whom he called his 'feline secretary' as she would sit on his manuscripts whilst he worked on them then move the pages out of his reach!*

*The Smoky Persian is very luxuriant.*

*The Chinchilla Longhair has large, expressive emerald-green eyes outlined in black or brown.*

## ~ 29 ~

## ~ 30 ~

## ~ 31 ~

### MYTHS & ORIGINS

#### Korat

Si-Sawat - meaning good fortune - is the name given to the Korat in its native Thailand. Much prized for their beauty, these sweet-tempered cats were described in ancient Thai manuscripts. Created by artists and writers of the Ayudha period (1350 - 1767 AD), these tell of a blue cat having 'hairs so smooth, with roots like clouds and tips like silver' and 'eyes that shine like dewdrops on a lotus leaf'. The clear, luminous eyes of the Korat are part of its mystique - 'These cloud coloured cats with eyes the colour of young rice…'

Symbols of good luck, Korats were often given to brides to ensure a happy and prosperous future. Originating hundreds of years ago in the Korat Province of Siam, now known as Thailand, the Korat today still possesses the same compact, muscular body, blue, silver-tipped coat and sparkling green eyes that intrigued and enchanted its countrymen all those years ago… The coat of some Korats, however, is of a deeper hue so as to be almost indigo. These rare and very special cats are known as 'black pearls…'

Then, as now, the Korat has a gentle nature with a marked dislike of noise. Their very sensitive hearing prompted the Thais to place them as 'watch-cats' in the temples, to guard the valuable treasures there.

The first Korat to be shown in England was probably in 1896 when a blue cat was entered in the Siamese class at the National Cat Club Show. Disqualified by judges who said the cat was 'blue instead of biscuit-coloured', its owner protested that not only had the cat come from Siam, but there were also many more like it! There was some confusion at this time surrounding the 'blue Siamese', and although blue self-coloured cats of Siamese type were mentioned in cat fancy literature, it was not until 1959 that the Korat was registered, when a pair named Nara and Darra were acquired from a breeder in Bangkok and taken to America.

*A rare and exotic breed, the Korat is silver-blue in colour and has large, luminous green eyes.*

# ~ *August* ~

'The cat makes himself the companion of your hours of solitude, melancholy and toil. He remains for whole evenings on your knee, uttering his contented purr, happy to be with you, and forsaking the company of animals of his own species. In vain do melodious mewings on the roof invite him to one of those cat parties in which fish bones play the part of tea and cakes; he is not to be tempted away from you. Put him down and he will jump up again, with a sort of cooing sound that is like a gentle reproach; and sometimes he will sit upon the carpet in front of you, looking at you with eyes so melting, so caressing, so human, that they almost frighten you; for it is impossible to believe that a soul is not there.'

Théophile Gautier, 1850

*August's cat is bold and proud with a big heart, and makes a loyal and generous companion.*

# ~ August ~

## ~ 1 ~

## ~ 2 ~

### CAT SNIPS

*August 2nd 1940: Thousands of signatures were obtained by Our Dumb Friends League on a petition calling for a taxation on cats. The League pointed out that a small tax on the six million cats in Great Britain could result in excess of £1 million towards the War Effort.*

## ~ 3 ~

## ~ 4 ~

### CAT SNIPS

*Tom, a cat belonging to the chief verger at Exeter Cathedral, was attacked by an owl as he killed a rat. On his death in 1950, a carving of Tom was mounted on a pillar in the chapel of the Cathedral.*

## ~ 5 ~

## ~ 6 ~

## ~ 7 ~

### PERSONALITY CATS

#### Louis Wain

*(b. 5th August 1860 - d. 4th July 1939)*

*Former teacher at the West London School of Art, dedicated cat lover and talented artist whose drawings, paintings and childrens' books highlighted the great popularity of the cat in Victorian and Edwardian England. At the age of 23, Wain married Emily Richardson and Peter, a small black and white kitten, became their beloved pet. When Emily fell terminally ill, Peter was her constant companion. Following the death of his wife, a distraught Wain produced a proliferation of acutely observed drawings and paintings featuring felines clothed in human attire and striking human attitudes in a unique and amusing way.*

*Elected President of the National Cat Club in 1890, Wain was also its Show Manager and a Judge, and designed the NCC logo which is still used today. Demand for his work increased until, on his return from a trip to America in 1910, a decline set in. The artist struggled on until 1924 when he was eventually certified insane. In 1939, Louis Wain died in hospital, leaving behind a rich legacy of work.*

*Kittens at play are very amusing.*

For show purposes, a Bicolour Persian should have evenly-distributed coloured patches with clear white patches to include the underside.

**RECORD-BREAKING CATS**
*The largest litter in the UK belonged to Burmese female Tara who, in 1970, gave birth to nineteen kittens.*

~ 8 ~

~ 9 ~

~ 10 ~

**CAT LEGENDS**
*A legend relates that when Noah built his Ark, he had two of every animal except the domestic cat, which was unknown at the time. The rain began to fall and the rats began to multiply and raid the Ark's store of provision. In despair, Noah asked the Lion for advice. The Lion thought, scratched his head and sneezed whereupon two small lions jumped out of his nostrils. These were the very first cats and they immediately began hunting, quickly diminishing the number of rats and mice.*

~ 11 ~

~ 12 ~

**CARTOON CATS**
*Figaro, a kitten, was created for Walt Disney's full-length film Pinocchio in 1940.*

~ 13 ~

~ 14 ~

*The ever-appealing Abyssinian.*

*Most cats keep their claws in good condition by 'stropping' on tree trunks or scratching posts. Others may need to have their's clipped.*

# ~ August ~

~ 15 ~

**CAT STARS**
*Solomon was a Chinchilla longhair
who became a movie star in such
films as 'Diamonds are Forever' and
'A Clockwork Orange'.*

~ 16 ~

~ 17 ~

~ 18 ~

**CAT FACTS**
*In Ancient Egypt, the male cat
represented the Sun and the female
cat, the Moon.*

~ 19 ~

~ 20 ~

~ 21 ~

*A Persian in deserved prime position.*

**CAT SNIPS**
*The origin of the Cheshire Cat
featured in Lewis Carroll's 'Alice in
Wonderland' is somewhat ambiguous
but there are two sources from which
the Cheshire-born author may have
based the character of the famous
disappearing cat. One concerns the
Cheshire town of Congleton, where
a ghostly cat unpredictably appeared
and disappeared, a phenomenon
witnessed by certain townsfolk
during the last century. The second
source concerns a medieval tale from
the City of Chester, wherein lived
one John Catterall, a landowner who
also was a forester. His skill with an
axe made him ideal for the post of
Public Executioner and Catterall
gained fame for the manner in which
he dispatched wrongdoers - with a
wide grin on his face. Appropriately,
his coat of arms displayed a grinning
cat.*

*In Britain, the Chinchilla differs from other Persians in that it is slightly more fine-boned, though it is no less hardy.*

# ~ August ~

~ 22 ~

~ 23 ~

~ 24 ~

### SUPERSTITIOUS CATS
*If the household cat sneezes near the
bride on her wedding morning, the
marriage will be a happy one.*

~ 25 ~

### CAT SNIPS
*'In the event of an air raid, don't
worry about your cats. Cats can
take care of themselves far better
than you can. Your cat will probably
meet you as you enter the air raid
shelter.' (From Hints on Household
ARP, an Autumn 1939 BBC radio
broadcast.)*

~ 26 ~

~ 27 ~

~ 28 ~

### PERSONALITY CATS

**Jean Michel Jarre**
*(b. 24th August 1948)
French musician and composer,
whose albums Oxygene and Equinox
are among his greatest hits, Jean
Michel Jarre lives in Paris with his
actress wife Charlotte Rampling.
Plus a large tabby cat called Woody -
named after screen comedy star
Woody Allen. Woody once had a
partner called Allen, but he
unfortunately disappeared after a
house move.*

*A fine example of the tabby.*

'Paws for thought' and a little nap on a cool flagstone.

# ~ August ~

## ~ 29 ~

## ~ 30 ~

## ~ 31 ~

### CAT BREEDS

#### Maine Coon

One of the oldest breeds of cat in America, the Maine Coon originated in the State of Maine and was first recorded in 1861 with mention of one called 'Captain Jenks'. Thought to be the result of matings between an Angora and Maine working cats, American folklore has it, because of the dark, tabby coat and bushy tail, that semi-wild cats mated with raccoons - hence the name, Maine Coon. Not unlike the Norwegian Forest Cat, the Main Coon is a hardy cat with a shaggy, semi-longhaired coat. It is also one of the largest of the cat breeds, weighing around 5 - 7kgs (11 - 15lbs) One example was said to weigh 18kgs (40lbs)! First exhibited in America in 1895, the Maine Coon is now a popular cat both in the US and the UK.

*According to American folklore, the impressive Main Coon is the result of a semi-wild cat and a racoon mating.*

*A beautiful Maine Coon with the breed's distinctively high cheek bones and pointed, tufted ears.*

# - *September* -

'Those fortunate enough to have been touched by its mystique will agree that once the strange Oriental magic of the Siamese cat has been revealed to them, they will forever remain in its enchanted spell...'

The Fabulous Siamese, Joan Moore, 1986

September's cat is fastidiously clean and hygienic and is not averse to its own company – the classic cat.

# ~ September ~

~ 1 ~

~ 2 ~

~ 3 ~

~ 4 ~

~ 5 ~

~ 6 ~

~ 7 ~

*Strong and massive, the handsome Chartreux.*

**CAT FACTS**

*Russian history tells us that long ago, in a magnificent palace in St. Petersburg, three hundred cats were kept to hunt and kill the mice that might otherwise destroy the many priceless leather-bound books which were stored in its library.*

**CAT SNIPS**

*Valued highly for their services to man, cats in China (5th century AD) were often given the name of Tama, meaning 'jewel'.*

## PERSONALITY CATS

### Colette
#### (1873 - 1954)

*A French authoress who adored cats, Colette wrote Claudine, the semi-autobiographical series of novels and also Cheri in 1920. In La Chatte (1933) the writer describes the tortures of jealousy when a young husband has eyes, and arms, only for Saha, his beloved cat. Camilla, the wife seeks to destroy the object of her husband's passion - and fails, only to lose her husband for ever... Saha, the feline heroine in the story is based on La Chatte, the cat which Colette and her husband Maurice Goudeket shared. La Chatte, a Chartreuse, was a delightful creature with a plushy blue coat and yellow eyes who selected her mistress at a cat show.*

*The many cats in Colette's works include the pampered La Belle Franchette, Babou, a black cat with a penchant for fruit and vegetables from the kitchen garden and her own Angora, Kiki-la-Doucette and French Bulldog Toby-Chien. Dialogue des Betes was a collection of 'conversations' between these two pets. Colette, the flamboyant cat-lover who posed as the Sphynx in a photograph which was thought to be both daring and controversial, said: 'There are no ordinary cats...'*

Virtually the same as the British Blue Shorthair, the Chartreux has a slightly more greyish blue coat.

# ~ September ~

~ 8 ~

## CARTOON CATS
*Lucifer, the spoiled house cat in Walt Disney's film 'Cinderella', is the scourge of the local mice.*

~ 9 ~

~ 10 ~

*Kittens are irrepressibly curious.*

## CAT STARS
*Frisky appears as the opening credits roll in Granada TV's long-running soap 'Coronation Street' - a story of everyday life in Manchester, England. Tabby and white Frisky leads a private life far removed from his 'Coronation Street' image, however, and resides in a stately home in Yorkshire with his own chauffered white Rolls Royce and a maid to see to his every need!*

~ 11 ~

~ 12 ~

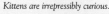

*Contact is very important for kittens.*

~ 13 ~

~ 14 ~

## CAT SNIPS
*'Last of all, but first in the catalogue and in point of the interest he excited, was Mr. L. Smith's tortoise-shell tom. He stood all alone in his glory. None but himself could be his parallel, and considering his rarity, the price fixed upon him (10/-) does not seem exorbitant.'*

The Graphic: *'Prize cats at the Crystal Palace'*

*At about a month of age a kitten, like a toddling child, will be in and out of everything.*

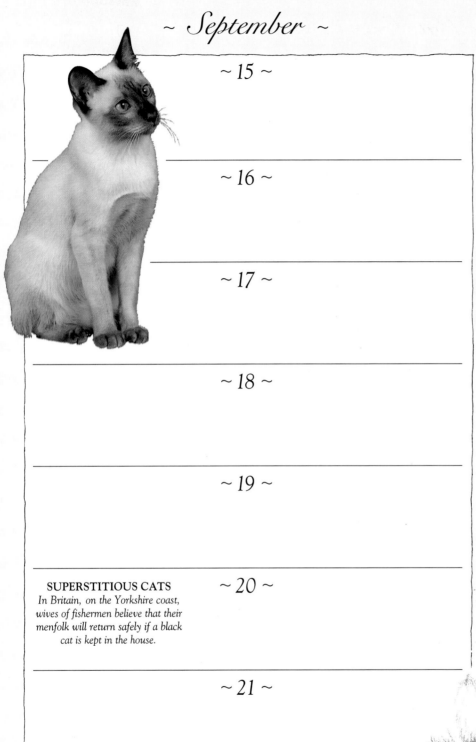

# ~ *September* ~

~ 15 ~

~ 16 ~

~ 17 ~

~ 18 ~

~ 19 ~

~ 20 ~

**SUPERSTITIOUS CATS**
*In Britain, on the Yorkshire coast, wives of fishermen believe that their menfolk will return safely if a black cat is kept in the house.*

~ 21 ~

**CAT SNIPS**
*Cardinal Richelieu (1585 - 1642) was so fond of cats that he shared his home with fourteen of them - their names included Pyramé, Thisbe, Lucifer and Perruque. Specially appointed attendants cared for the cats and on his death, the Cardinal left all his worldly wealth to his feline companions.*

**CATS WITH CONNECTIONS**
*Humphrey joined the staff of No. 10 Downing Street in September 1989 after walking in off the street. He was named after Sir Humphrey, a character in the television programme 'Yes Minister'.*

*The Tonkinese is a cross between a Siamese and a Burmese, developed in America in the 1970s.*

# ~ September ~

~ 22 ~

~ 23 ~

~ 24 ~

~ 25 ~

### SUPERSTITIOUS CATS
*When a cat washes its face in the parlour, company can be expected.*

~ 26 ~

~ 27 ~

~ 28 ~

## PERSONALITY CATS

### Brigitte Bardot
*(b. 28th September 1934)*
President of the Bardot Foundation and cult film star of the 'Fifties, Brigitte Bardot created a glamorous 'pouting' image which was copied worldwide and which earned her the title of 'sex kitten'. A long-time resident of St. Tropez in the South of France, Bardot has now given her life to the welfare of animals upon which practically all of her personal wealth has been spent. She shares her large, rambling home with many stray cats and dogs.

## PERSONALITY CATS

### Thomas Stearns Eliot
*(b. 26th September 1888 - d. January 1965)*
Born in St. Louis, Missouri, TS Eliot was the youngest of seven children in a family of English origin who had emigrated to Massachussetts from Somerset, England in the 17th century. Educated at Harvard, the Sorbonne in Paris and at Merton College, Oxford, TS Eliot finally settled in England.

Meeting his contemporary, Ezra Pound, Eliot became interested in the theatre and wrote plays - notably Murder in the Cathedral, commissioned for the Canterbury Festival of 1935. Verse featured strongly in his literary career and, reflecting his passion for cats, Old Possum's Book of Practical Cats appeared in 1939. Eliot's wife ·Valerie recalls that he was always inventing suitable cat names and remembers Noilly Prat - an elegant cat - and Tantomile - a witch's cat... Published on 5th October 1939 with his own drawings on the front cover and dust jacket, Old Possum's Book of Practical Cats became a best-seller worldwide and was translated into many languages. TS Eliot received the Order of Merit in 1948 and the Nobel Prize for Literature in that same year.

*A proud Persian of great charisma.*

*This Red-and-White Bicolour Longhair's disarmingly open gaze makes it quite irresistible.*

# ~ September ~

## ~ 29 ~

## ~ 30 ~

The Norwegian Forest Cat.

A breed of great distinction.

Used to harsh Scandinavian winters, this cat has a thick double coat.

## MYTHS & ORIGINS

### Norwegian Forest Cat

An active, athletic cat giving the impression of great power and strength, the Norwegian Forest Cat is a natural breed which features prominently in Scandinavian folklore. It is said that long, long ago this large and fearsome cat of the northern forests was taken by the Vikings to guard their homes and to live alongside their families as vermin-hunters and household pets. It is also said that these longhaired cats were carried on the shoulders of the Vikings as they rode into battle, to attack and claw the faces of their enemies. Many old Scandinavian folk tales, though often confused and compounded, featured these felines who were much respected by the Norsemen for their strength and agility. That the marauding Vikings took these cats on their voyages to the known world and beyond is also held to be true. As the Norwegian Forest Cat bears a strong resemblance to the Maine Coon in the US, this could indicate the extent of the sea-going forays of the Norsemen.

In Norse mythology, the chariot of Freya, goddess of beauty, love and fertility, is drawn by two large, longhaired cats - these creatures are often connected with powers of creativity, Earth-Mother and fertility goddesses. Also connected with Freya is Utgard-Loki, King of the Giants who also had one such giant cat. The Norwegian Forest Cat, or Norsk Skaukatt, is probably the main character in Scandinavia's own version of 'Puss in Boots' in which the ogre is a troll - in mythology, trolls die in the sunlight - so that to help its master, this resourceful puss kept the troll chatting throughout the night, letting the early morning sunlight destroy him...

*Similar in appearance to the Maine Coon, the Norwegian Forest Cat may be of various colours.*

# ~ *October* ~

'When we go into the likeness of a cat, we say thrice over:

"I shall go into a cat,
With sorrow and a sigh and a black shot.
I shall go in the Devil's name
Ay, while I come home again".'

Magick Spell used for Metamorphosis as described by the witch
Isabel Gowdie at her trial in Scotland in 1662

*October's cat loves the finer things in life like soft cushions, gentle music and constant shows of affection.*

# ~ October ~

~ 1 ~

~ 2 ~

**PRESIDENTIAL CATS**
Born in 1924, Jimmy Carter's
Presidential feline friend was Misty
Malarky Ying Yang, a male Siamese
pet cat of his daughter, Amy Carter.

~ 3 ~

~ 4 ~

~ 5 ~

**SUPERSTITIOUS CATS**
It is said that a cat looking out of the
window is looking for rain.

~ 6 ~

~ 7 ~

**CAT SNIPS**
A sensible quote from 19th century
British cat expert Frances Simpson,
discussing the newly imported
Siamese cat: 'Siamese are a special
breed and should be kept as such -
the same may be said of the Manx
and the Blues. All attempts to cross
these cats with other breeds should be
discouraged.'

*A fine litter of Birman kittens.*

*The appealing face of the Siamese.*

*The quintessential Siamese – the seal point. The pale fawn to cream body is marked at the tail, feet, legs, mask and ears.*

*A cat makes a home.*

~ 8 ~

~ 9 ~

~ 10 ~

~ 11 ~

~ 12 ~

~ 13 ~

~ 14 ~

### CAT SNIPS

*Kasper is a wooden black cat, designed by Basil Ionides in 1916, which stands on a shelf in the Pinafore Room in London's prestigious Savoy Hotel. When guests at a luncheon or dinner party number thirteen, Kasper is placed on a chair before the fourteenth place, thus confounding the superstition that thirteen seated at table is unlucky. Winston Churchill frequently dined in this room and on several occasions when his party numbered thirteen, he asked for Kasper to be placed at the table.*

### SUPERSTITIOUS CATS

In America, black and white and also grey cats are considered to be lucky.

### CATS WITH CONNECTIONS

*Margate was a black kitten that turned up on the doorstep of No. 10 Downing Street and was taken in on October 10th 1953, the day of Prime Minister Winston Churchill's speech to the Conservatives at Margate.*

*Shampooed, groomed and back-lit, this Persian has been bred for stardom.*

# ~ October ~

## CAT STARS

*MTM Kitten is a corporate mascot with an unknown name. This little tabby appears in the logo of MTM (Mary Tyler Moore) Enterprises Inc. television production company which was first used in 1970.*

*The very elegant Cat of Bengal.*

**~ 15 ~**

**~ 16 ~**

**~ 17 ~**

**~ 18 ~**

**~ 19 ~**

## CAT SNIPS

*When the 6th century Pope Gregory the First retired to a monastery for a period of time, he took with him a cat as his companion.*

**~ 20 ~**

**~ 21 ~**

*A lithe and agile breed.*

## PERSONALITY CATS

***Actress Sandra Dickinson***
*(b. 20th October in Washington DC)*
*Mainly cast in 'dizzy blonde' type roles, Sandra starred in such TV films as The Hitch-hikers' Guide to the Galaxy, The Clairvoyant and the US TV series Eisenhower and Lutz. Sandra is married to actor Peter Davison and they have a daughter called Georgia and four cats.*

*With its 'big cat' appearance the Cat of Bengal is an impressive animal of surprisingly good nature.*

# ~ October ~

## ~ 22 ~

### SUPERSTITIOUS CATS
*It is unlucky to hear a cat crying before setting off on a journey. If this happens, return and find out what it wants.*

## ~ 23 ~

## ~ 24 ~

## ~ 25 ~

## ~ 26 ~

## ~ 27 ~

### PRESIDENTIAL CATS
*'Teddy' Roosevelt, born this day in 1858, enjoyed the company of a cat called Slippers while residing at the White House. Slippers was a grey (blue) cat and was what is known as polydactyl, which means that he had more than the usual five toes on his front paws!*

## ~ 28 ~

*Cats always land on their feet.*

*A British Shorthair and kitten.*

*The British Shorthair has large, widely spaced eyes of arresting directness set in a handsome, round face.*

# ~ October ~

## CAT SNIPS

Micetto, a large blue and red tabby cat, was born in the Vatican and raised by Pope Leo XII.

## ~ 29 ~

## ~ 30 ~

## ~ 31 ~

## CAT SNIPS

All Hallowes E'en is celebrated on 31st October. A pagan feast of the dead and marking the moment when supernatural forces symbolizing cold and death return to Earth, witches and warlocks, accompanied by their feline 'familiars', travel on broomsticks to the great Sabbats. Followers of the path of Wicca call this night Samhain…

## CAT BREEDS

### Manx

The tailless Manx is a native of the Isle of Man, an island steeped in ancient Celtic folklore and situated mid-way between England and Ireland. Legend has it that invaders of the island cut off the tails of the Manx cats to decorate their helmets. Mother cats, anxious to save their kittens from harm, bit off their tails at birth until eventually, the kittens were born tailless. Whilst it is also maintained that the Manx were transported from Japan to the British Isles by Phoenician traders, the most probable origin is that in 1558, a ship from the Spanish Armada was shipwrecked off the coast of the Isle of Man and tailless cats on board swam ashore to become the ancestors of the present day Manx.

A Manx Cat Club was formed in 1901 and King Edward VII was known to have several of these cats as pets. The Manx can be seen in three stages of 'taillessness'. The 'rumpy', completely tailless; the 'stumpy' and the 'longie' each show residual tails of varying lengths. The 'rumpy' possesses a lethal factor in that the kittens of two 'rumpy' parents are often stillborn.

*The Manx cat.*

The Manx has a solid, stocky frame and a distinctively rounded rump and, of course, little or no tail.

# - *November* -

'A cat should be handled gently and kept as calm as possible during the judging. Women are naturally more gentle in their methods, and more tender-hearted. When my pets are entered in competition, may some wise, kind woman have the judging of them!'

Helen Winslow, 1900

*November's cat is deeply emotional and should be treated with great care if harmony is to be established.*

# ~ November ~

~ 1 ~

~ 2 ~

~ 3 ~

~ 4 ~

~ 5 ~

~ 6 ~

~ 7 ~

## CAT STARS

*Tao was the male Siamese cat appearing in 'The Incredible Journey' (1961) from the book by Sheila Burnford, and who, along with his dog companions, undertook a long, adventurous journey to find his master.*

## CAT SNIPS

*Note for show cats… Siamese cats kept in high temperature conditions will produce a lighter, more desirable coat. Conversely, a drop in temperature produces a much darker coat colour.*

## PERSONALITY CATS

### Vivien Leigh

*(b. 5th November 1913 - d. 8th July 1967)*

*British stage and screen star, famous for her feline type of grace and beauty, Vivien Leigh won Academy Awards for Best Actress 1939 for her role as Scarlett O'Hara in Gone With the Wind and as Blanche du Bois in Tennessee Williams' Streetcar Named Desire in 1951. Vivien Leigh and her then husband Sir Laurence Olivier owned two seal point Siamese males, Boy and New. The cats travelled by Vivien's side whenever she went on tour. New was named after the New Theatre in London, with which she and Sir Laurence were so closely connected.*

*A playful Seal Point Siamese kitten.*

Narrow and delicate, the Siamese is an instantly recognizable breed and one of the most popular pedigrees.

~ 8 ~

~ 9 ~

**SUPERSTITIOUS CATS**
No cat which has been bought will
ever be any good at catching mice.

~ 10 ~

~ 11 ~

~ 12 ~

**CAT SNIPS**
In the 9th century, King Henry 1 of
Saxony decreed that the fine for
killing a cat should be sixty bushels of
corn.

~ 13 ~

~ 14 ~

**PERSONALITY CATS**

*Claude Rains*
(b. 10th November 1889 - d. 30th
May 1967)
An English-born character actor of
stage and screen, Claude Rains'
most famous roles were in American
films. Though mainly cast in sinister-
type parts, one of his best-known
was the title role of Caesar in Caesar
and Cleopatra. In this late 'Forties
technicolour record-breaker directed
by Cecil B de Mille, Claude Rains
played opposite a 'kittenish' Vivien
Leigh - a fitting part for an actor
renowned throughout Hollywood as
a dedicated cat person.

*Hunter amongst the hunted.*

*The Angora is named after Ankara in Turkey, from where it originates, and makes an affectionate, playful pet.*

# ~ November ~

~ 15 ~

**CARTOON CATS**

*Duchess is the elegant Parisian cat who features in Walt Disney Productions' animated feature 'The Aristocats' in 1970. She is abducted to the French countryside where she meets a Dickensian assortment of animal characters and persuades O'Malley the alley cat to help her escape back home.*

~ 16 ~

~ 17 ~

*A classically-proportioned puss.*

**SUPERSTITIOUS CATS**

*Indonesians and Malays believe that if you wash your cat it will bring rain.*

~ 18 ~

~ 19 ~

*The pretty California Spangled Cat.*

~ 20 ~

~ 21 ~

The large, appealing eyes of the California Spangled Cat are defined by fine black rims.

# ~ November ~

~ 22 ~

~ 23 ~

The nonchalantly beautiful Colourpoint.

~ 24 ~

~ 25 ~

**CAT SNIPS**
Dr. Samuel Johnson, the 17th century diarist, was particularly devoted to his cat Hodge. When James Boswell, friend and biographer of Samuel Johnson - and ailurophobe - noted with distaste his friend's close affinity with his cat, he remarked with some reservation that Hodge was a very fine cat. Johnson replied that yes he was, but that he had owned even finer cats than Hodge. Fearing the disapproval of his feline friend, he hastily added 'But he is a very fine cat, a very fine cat indeed!'

**CAT FACTS**
The following extraordinary extract appeared in the Japan Daily Herald on 26th November 1877: 'In order to escape cholera, the dogs in the Matsushima neighbourhood, the cats and birds in Horiye, the monkeys and bears in Nambajinchi, the rabbits in the Temma Temple and the deer in the Sakuranomiya Temple are wearing charms'.

~ 26 ~

~ 27 ~

**RECORD-BREAKING CATS**
Puss from Devon was probably the oldest male cat ever recorded. He died the day after his 36th birthday which was 28th November 1939.

~ 28 ~

*The Colourpoint, or Himalayan, makes an extremely good house cat of great personal charm.*

## ~ 29 ~

---

### PRESIDENTIAL CATS

*Born this day in 1835, Mark Twain described a cat called Tom Quartz in his story, 'Roughing It', a name later bestowed upon the first feline of the Theodore Roosevelt administration.*

## ~ 30 ~

### PERSONALITY CATS

**Rt. Hon. Winston Spencer Churchill**
*(b. 30th November 1874 - d. 24th January 1965)*
*Winston Churchill, former war correspondent in the First World War and Prime Minister of Great Britain during the Second World War, owned a cat named Jock who attended many war-time Cabinet meetings. Rumour has it that meals in the Churchill household did not commence until 'ginger' tabby Jock was present at the table.*

*The long-necked California Spangled Cat.*

*The feline will habitually find a place that's 'safe' for its infamous naps. Roofs, windowsills and walls all suffice.*

# ~ *December* ~

I like little pussy, her coat is so warm;
And if I don't hurt her, she'll do me no harm.
So I'll not pull her tail, nor drive her away,
But pussy and I very gentle will play.
She shall sit by my side, and I'll give her some food;
And she'll love me because I am gentle and good.

I'll pat pretty pussy, and then she will purr;
And thus show her thanks for my kindness to her.
But I'll not pinch her ears, nor tread on her paw,
Lest I should provoke her to use her sharp claw.
I never will vex her, nor make her displeased -
For pussy don't like to be worried and teased.

Anon, c.1830

*The December cat is a happy-go-lucky puss that will prove a diligent mouser and entertaining character.*

# ~ *December* ~

~ 1 ~

**SUPERSTITIOUS CATS**
*In Western Europe it is widely
believed that if a cat washes over its
ears it is a sign of rain.*

~ 2 ~

**CARTOON CATS**
*Top Cat was created in 1961 by
Hanna-Barbera. Top Cat, the truly
cool alley cat, has been enjoyed by
numerous children.*

~ 3 ~

~ 4 ~

~ 5 ~

~ 6 ~

*A delightful Golden Persian.*

~ 7 ~

Gentle, friendly cats – Somalis make good parents as well as pets and are highly commended for their good looks.

# ~ December ~

## CAT SNIPS

*William, a white cat of which 19th century English author Charles Dickens was particularly fond, was re-christened Williamina when her kittens were born!*

### ~ 8 ~

### ~ 9 ~

*Good breeding shows in these Chinchillas.*

### ~ 10 ~

### ~ 11 ~

## SUPERSTITIOUS CATS

*When cats rush about wildly, clawing at curtains and cushions, it means that wind is coming.*

### ~ 12 ~

### ~ 13 ~

### ~ 14 ~

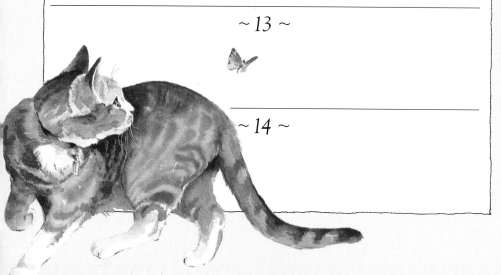

## PERSONALITY CATS

### Edward G. Robinson
*(b. 12th December 1893 - d. 26th January 1973)*

*A Hollywood star of stage and screen and noted for his 'tough guy' roles, Edward G Robinson is well-remembered for his portrayal of gangsters in such films as 'Little Caesar, Double Indemnity, Hell on 'Frisco Bay and latterly the science-fiction thriller Soylent Green in 1973. In private life, a cultured man who spoke eight languages, Edward G. was also the devoted owner of a Siamese cat, often seen draped across the lap of its owner by the pool at his luxurious Hollywood home.*

*Longhaired cats who enjoy the outdoors will be time-consuming pets as their coats will get very tangled.*

~ 15 ~

~ 16 ~

**SUPERSTITIOUS CATS**
*When cats sit with their back to the fire, look out for frost or a storm.*

~ 17 ~

~ 18 ~

**CAT SNIPS**
*According to legend, the 'M' marking on the forehead of the tabby cat was created by the prophet Mahomet as he rested his hand lightly on the brow of his favourite cat...*

~ 19 ~

~ 20 ~

~ 21 ~

**PERSONALITY CATS**
*Betty Grable*
*(b. 18th December 1916 - d. 2nd July 1973)*
*A popular actress, dancer and singer, Grable's famed legs danced their way through such 'Forties films as The Diamond Horseshoe, The Dolly Sisters and Mother Wore Tights. Married and divorced from one-time child star Jackie Coogan and bandleader Harry James, Betty Grable was devoted to cats and allowed her own to wander through her Hollywood home at will.*

*Tabby cat and bronze.*

*The European Shorthair comes in many different coat and colour combinations and this dramatic silver and black tabby is most impressive.*

# ~ December ~

## ~ 22 ~

## ~ 23 ~

**CAT SNIPS**
*On Christmas Eve, according to folklore from the English Cotswolds, cats can be conversed with - if addressed in rhyme.*

## ~ 24 ~

## ~ 25 ~

**SUPERSTITIOUS CATS**
*A black cat in the audience on opening night portends a successful play.*

## ~ 26 ~

## ~ 27 ~

## ~ 28 ~

*Who knows what cats think of?*

**PERSONALITY CATS**

***Humphrey Bogart***
*(b. 25th December 1899 - d. 14th January 1957)*
*Born Humphrey deForest Bogart in New York City, Bogart was a popular stage and screen star who specialised in 'tough guy' roles. He won Academy Awards for Casablanca (1942), The African Queen (1951) and The Caine Mutiny (1954). Married four times and latterly to actress Lauren Bacall, with whom he lived happily until his death, Humphrey Bogart was a confirmed cat lover.*

**CARTOON CATS**
*Tom the alley cat starred in 154 cartoons with his co-star, Jerry the Mouse. These two popular characters were created by William Hanna and Joseph Barbera. Seven of the cartoons won Oscars.*

*This appealing Silver Somali kitten is quite a little charmer!*

# ~ December ~

## ~ 29 ~

## ~ 30 ~

## ~ 31 ~

### PERSONALITY CATS

#### Rudyard Kipling
(b. 30th December 1865 - d. 18th January 1936)
An English story writer and poet whose intuitive works often reflect his links with 19th century India and the British Raj, Rudyard Kipling was particularly sensitive with regard to the cat. In The Cat That Walked by Himself from the Just So stories, Kipling succeeds in summing up the feline psyche: 'I am not a friend, and I am not a servant. I am the Cat that walks by himself and I wish to come into your cave.'

The Turkish Van, an unusual breed.

## MYTHS & ORIGINS

#### Angora & Turkish Van

At the end of the sixteenth century, the Angora cat arrived in Europe. Brought first to France by scientist Claude Fabri de Peirese, this lovely cat originated in the Turkish city of Angora - now known as Ankara. Much admired for its long silky coat and quiet, graceful charm, the Angora's body was long, slender and of 'oriental' type. An English writer in 1868 describes the Angora as a 'beautiful variety with silvery hair of fine texture, generally longest on the neck but also on the tail'. The white variety of the Angora was often felt to be the only true representative of the breed and consequently Ankara Zoo established a breeding colony of whites.

In its native homeland, the Angora is known by other names - according to colour. For instance, the red tabby variety is known as the sarman; the silver tabby is the teku and the odd-eyed white is known as Ankara kedi. Another true-breeding variety which evolved within the Angora breed was the Turkish Van. Living high in the mountainous regions of Lake Van, these cats were white with an attractive 'auburn' colouring restricted to ears and tail. Understandably perhaps, the Van was an expert swimmer - earning the name of The Swimming Cat in Turkey, its country of origin.

A litter of Turkish Vans before the appearance of their auburn patching.

Most unusually, the Turkish Van enjoys playing in water and sheds a great deal of its coat in the summer.

# ~ *Aquarius* ~

(January 21st - February 19th)
*The sign of the WATER BEARER*

*Tolerant, reserved, idealistic*

*Resembling the Capricornian cat in its dependability when the influence of Saturn is strong, the Aquarian cat becomes extrovert and rebellious when the influence of Uranus prevails. There is, therefore, an unpredictability factor to this cat which is most disconcerting. More intelligent than the average feline, this one remains unperturbed in moments of crisis, consequently making a born leader with a singular sense of vision - attributable to the third all-seeing eye which is said to be invisibly lodged in the middle of the Aquarian forehead. In Egyptian mythology this is called the Eye of Horus.*

*A seeker of truth (key word: I know), the Aquarian cat is a dab hand (paw) at the old 'penetrating looks' ploy and meeting its cold calculating eye can be an edifying experience for its all too human owner. All is not such an uncomfortable ride as would at first appear, however, as the positive traits to the nature of the Aquarian cat are that it can be caring, intuitive (!), friendly, loyal and trustworthy. Often of slender build with widely spaced eyes and pointed ears, health problems are connected with the legs, teeth, general circulation and nervous system. Guard against damage to ankles, toothache and gum disease.*

**Compatible signs:** *Libra and Gemini*

# ~ *Pisces* ~

(February 20th - March 20th)
*The sign of the FISH*

*Imaginative, peace-loving and kind*

*Pisces is the twelfth and last sign of the Zodiac. The dreamy Piscean cat is an idealist and unless constantly reminded otherwise, will exist in a fantasy world of its own making. Imaginative and warm-hearted, these delightful creatures are among life's 'gentle folk', full of understanding and forgiveness and far too 'nice' for this wicked world! The feline Piscean will avoid awkward situations like the plague, veering into the warm security of sunnier, trouble-free waters.*

*It dislikes criticism and will refuse to admit that it was the culprit who missed the litter tray, firmly convincing itself that some other cat was the guilty party. Often in agonies of indecision, this unhappy state of affairs tends to be a problem to the Piscean puss who will procrastinate and delay the evil moment when choices simply have to be made. Notwithstanding, this little cat with its small, shapely body and luminous eyes can achieve an almost psychic relationship with its owner or, less esoterically, can be the most sympathetic and supportive of companions. Two fishes swimming in opposite directions is the traditional Piscean symbol. It is not surprising, therefore, that the Piscean cat often takes to water quite easily. Pisces rules the feet, liver and circulation. Guard against cat 'flu and diseases of the liver.*

**Compatible signs:** *Cancer and Scorpio*

# ~ *Aries* ~

*(March 21st - April 20th)*
*The sign of the RAM*

*New beginnings, energy, leadership*

*Aries is the first sign of the Zodiac and the Arian cat typifies the glorious sense of awakening, rebirth and joyousness connected with the Vernal Equinox. He is courageous, volatile, assertive - and a dedicated lover! The male Arian cat is the eternal 'ginger tom from next door' whilst the female of the species is a flighty feline temptress. Both impossible flirts, each possess a fiery temper - understandable since Aries is a Fire sign - and the sparks will fly when the object of the male Arian's desire cries off with a headache!*

*Physically very active, the Arian cat shows a fine disregard for its owners treasured ornaments which may come to grief during a sudden fit of indoor gymnastics. This is a cat of energetic demeanour and with a quick, darting appearance. Tending towards lean and wiry and with a long slender neck, the Arian cat often manifests its Fire sign associations with a red or ruddy coat colour. Health problems most likely are those connected with the head, brain, upper jaw and carotid arteries. Guard against eye troubles, toothache and feverish sickness such as cat 'flu.*

**Compatible signs:** *Leo and Sagittarius.*

# ~ *Taurus* ~

*(April 21st - May 21st)*
*The sign of the BULL*

*Steadfast, courageous and firm*

*The Taurean cat is a good old-fashioned puss cat. Flighty this one is not - preferring domestic bliss and home comforts to naughty nights out on the tiles! Too many 'home comforts' however lead to a typically sturdy Taurean physique, therefore appetite should be carefully monitored to avoid obesity. More territorially minded than most, this cat fiercely defends its own back yard against all comers and the formidable Taurean frame with fur furiously 'bushed' is sufficient to discourage the most determined intruder.*

*Solidly built with bull-like neck and powerful shoulders, the manner of the Taurean is ponderous and its gait slow and deliberate. But make no mistake, in pursuance of sensual gratification - attributable to ruling planet Venus - and having attached itself to hearth, home (and board) of its humans, this feline will be a loyal and dependable friend for life. Positive traits of the Taurean cat are those of compassion, trustworthiness and practicality. Negative traits are jealousy, possessiveness and self-indulgence. There is also a tendency to attach too much significance to conservative ideas - hence a lack of flair and imagination! Vulnerable parts of the body are the neck, throat, ears and the back of the head. Guard against throat infections and obesity.*

**Compatible signs:** *Virgo and Capricorn*

# ~ Gemini ~

# ~ Cancer ~

*(May 22nd - June 21st)*
The sign of the TWINS

*Duality, versatility, the intellect*

*Exuberant and energetic, the Geminian cat is the quintessential 'playful pussy' with a mental dexterity which makes this cat the ideal companion for a like-minded human. Versatile and adaptable, this busy little feline is a great conversationalist and its vivacious chirruping could well charm birds, traditionally associated with this sign, out of trees! Graceful in build with quick, darting eyes, the Geminian cat is constantly active with a nervous energy springing from a seemingly endless source. Not surprising that Mercury, quicksilver messenger of the gods, is Gemini's ruling planet.*

*Gracious and charming but preferring to orchestrate relationships on its own terms, the Gemini cat is not a 'cuddly' little creature and can sometimes be a puzzling, enigmatic soul reflecting the duality of its birth sign. A love of open spaces and fresh air also echoes the Mutable-Air sign of the planet Gemini. The chatty little Gemini cat, however, can cause complete chaos with its restless romping around the home. Plants are ravaged, curtains climbed, knick-knacks knocked over and whose are those claw marks on the coffee table? Though usually making a swift recovery from most illnesses, health problems are experienced with the legs, shoulders and lungs.*

*(June 22nd - July 23rd)*
The sign of the CRAB

*Sensitive, maternal and very romantic*

*The Cancerian cat makes for a highly domesticated and dedicated home-loving feline - if female, the perfect Mum Cat. Unless destined to become a breeding queen or the male, a stud cat, the responsible owner is recommended to consider spaying or neutering, since nothing short of this will convince the Cancerian cat that it was not born to proliferate. Neutering, however, will not diminish this cat's kindly concern for all small furries. On the contrary, its strong maternal instinct will extend to other family pets who could find themselves borne off to the warm, comfortable nest of the Cancerian cat. For these concerned caring folk are the feline equivalent of the human 'lovely person'.*

*Ruled by the Moon and therefore often over-sensitive and vulnerable to the negative effects of dis-harmony, they are generally plump and cuddly with kind sweet expressions set in round, moon-like faces. Cancer rules the stomach so that these cats are prone to digestive upsets - particularly during times of stress. Guard against stomach ulcers, problems with the female reproductive organs and illnesses which require special diets.*

**Compatible signs:** *Libra and Aquarius*

**Compatible signs:** *Pisces and Scorpio.*

# ~ Leo ~

*(July 24th - August 23rd)*
*The sign of the LION*

*Self-confidence, enthusiasm, pride*

Flamboyant, big-hearted and with a strong sense of dignity, the leonine Leo cat can certainly equate with the title 'The King of Cats'. Demanding lots and lots of attention - and generally getting it – these fulsome Leo traits can often become negative to produce a vain, arrogant and domineering cat. Whilst traditionally Leo cats sport luxuriant coats of red or gold, not all of these splendid creatures possess the brilliant colours of their ruling planet the Sun. Coat condition of most Leo cats, however, is often quite spectacular.

These felines usually make excellent parents - the male a proud, protective father and the female, a wise and caring mother. Leo will always repay the love and attention received from its adoring owner (subject) with generosity, loyalty and a rare companionship until the end of its days. The bearing of the Leo cat is bold, regal and fearless. Its eyes are large, bright and impress all with their authoritative gaze. Leo cats are prone to heart and circulatory problems with a possibility of anaemia. Guard against diseases of the spine.

**Compatible signs:** *Aries and Sagittarius*

# ~ Virgo ~

*(August 24th - September 23rd)*
*The sign of the VIRGIN*

*Discriminative, methodical, logical*

The cat, thought of as a feminine animal, is usually associated with the astrological sign of Virgo. Certainly, this fastidiously clean, intelligent puss, often applying a fine sense of logic to achieve its own ends - plus lashings of laid-back charm – sums up most succinctly the Virgoan character. Compulsive coat and whisker washers, the Virgoan cat is an independent character who appreciates delicately prepared and regular meals.

A real cool cat who is not particularly demonstrative, this puss likes his or her own space and often exhibits a painstaking fastidiousness regarding its health and hygiene. This can pave the way to a downright 'finicky' cat. If this does occur, tempt the fussy feeder with small, frequent and tasty meals. If mealtimes are still angst-ridden, make sure that the small, frequent and tasty meals also involve deliciously inviting aromas. The independent character of this agreeable cat, plus a subdued sense of adventure, make the Virgoan feline a good choice for the career person. Parts of the Virgoan puss most prone to infection are the bowels, intestines and abdomen. Guard against diarrhoea and treat regularly for worms.

**Compatible signs:** *Capricorn and Taurus*

# ~ Libra ~

(September 24th - October 23rd)
The sign of the SCALES

*Balance, justice, love of beauty*

Lovers of harmony and peace, the Libran cat is intelligent, charming and makes a fine, sensitive companion - tuning in beautifully to its owner's every mood. Venus, goddess of love and beauty, is the ruling planet of Libra and accordingly exerts a somewhat sybaritic influence over this cat. Which can be observed in its appreciation of soft, melodious music and certain creature comforts - like the warmth and softness of its owner's bed!

A compulsive craver of comfort with just a touch of winsome appeal and 'cuddliness' make these cats ideal companions for the lonely. However, a well-balanced, sensitive soul such as this, oft given to contemplation of its clean little paws, the universe and everything, may occasionally allow itself to descend into bouts of negative thinking - despondency often alternating with fits of excitable elation, tipping the Libran's normally well-adjusted mental balance. Generally of slender and graceful proportions, the Libran cat is prone to kidney diseases, diabetic conditions and skin complaints, such as eczema, and others of an eruptive nature. Guard against skin complaints by ensuring that diet is not at fault.

**Compatible signs:** *Aquarius and Gemini*

# ~ Scorpio ~

(October 24th - November 22nd)
The sign of the SCORPION

*Tenacious, secretive, intensely psychic*

The Scorpio cat has boundless energy, great strength of purpose and its actions are often motivated by the depth of its passions. Being of an intensely emotional nature, this aspect of the Scorpio cat's character, if denied, can result in a creature of almost satanic intensity. Secretive and with piercing eyes that seem to seek out their owner's innermost fears, the Scorpio cat is the feline most likely to have been the 'familiar' of witches in medieval times.

Great manipulators, cats born under this sign appear to have everything under control - including their bemused owners (beware not to fall entirely under the spell of this cat!) Heavy, muscular and strong-boned, Scorpio cats are fiendishly adaptable and by some strange alchemy manage to exist on their own terms in most situations with very little trouble at all. Radiating a strong personal magnetism, cats born under this sign are both cautious yet courageous. But on the distaff side, the negative Scorpio feline is jealous, vindictive and some might think a likely candidate for re-homing! Scorpio rules the genital organs, the bladder and the colon. Guard against ulcers and hernias.

**Compatible signs:** *Cancer and Pisces*

# ~ Sagittarius ~

(November 23rd - December 21st)
The sign of the ARCHER

*Extrovert, optimistic, independent*

Sporty and with a well-developed sense of adventure, the Sagittarian cat is a happy-go-lucky feline surviving often 'more by good luck than by good management'. This cat's abundant energy coupled with its 'mis'guided missile approach to life make it a highly lovable character. The light-hearted, travel-happy attitude of the Sagittarian puss brings to mind Top Cat, the cartoon alley cat with a talent for getting into - and out of - numerous scrapes and still ending up with a smile on his face!

Given the opportunity, the Sagittarian cat is an excellent mouser and should its territory prove to be a mouse-free zone, its attention will turn to other quarries. Old crisp packets, socks, small toys - all these trophies and more are carried back home as loving gifts for the delight (?) of its human. Of athletic build with large, expressive eyes, the adventurous Sagittarian puss loves to be the centre of attention and because of its active lifestyle is more prone to accidents than most. Rheumatism - shades of those cold, damp nights on the tiles - is also a common complaint with this group. Guard against these problems by calling a curfew. Cosy nights by the fireside may convince this travelling cat that home is best.

**Compatible signs:** *Aries and Leo*

# ~ Capricorn ~

(December 22nd - January 20th)
The sign of the GOAT

*Industrious, meticulous, persevering*

Quiet and self-disciplined with an air of solidity and staidness gives the Capricornian cat a maturity beyond its years. Even Capricornian kittens are solemn little creatures, lacking the skittishness of their peers in other astrological groups. The Capricornian association with Father Time and old age is the key. Averse to change, this cat is also very cautious, preferring the security of its own territory indoors to the insecurity of the great outdoors. Said to be ruled by Saturn, the Great Taskmaster of the Zodiac, the Capricornian cat is living proof that you can put old heads on young shoulders!

The element Earth, with its traditional association with caves, is strong in the Capricornian make-up accounting for the somewhat restrained attitude of this cat. For, whilst the Capricorn cat makes a loyal and steadfast companion, it does not bestow its affections lightly. Long-bodied and with a straight nose in an angular face, problems afflicting this sign are rheumatism, cramp and a tendency to the dislocation of bones. Skin complaints such as eczema are common. Guard against these with careful dietary planning. Also guard against toothache.

**Compatible signs:** *Taurus and Virgo*